A Kid's Guide to Drawing™

How to Draw Cartoon Fish

Curt Visca and Kelley Visca

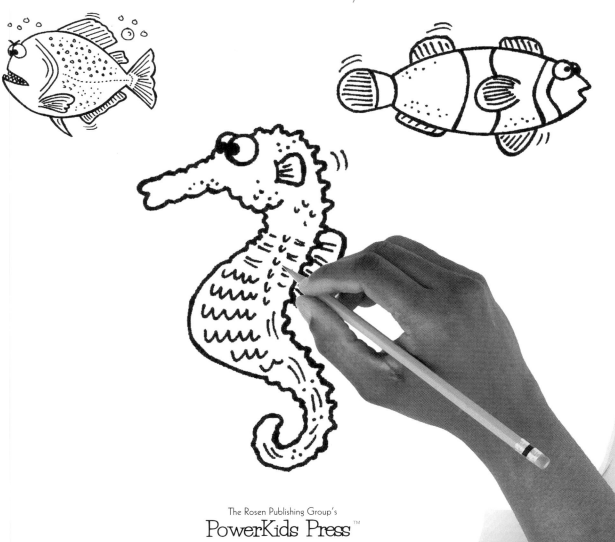

The Rosen Publishing Group's
PowerKids Press™
New York

Dedicated to the Lord for blessing us with God-given talent

Published in 2003 by The Rosen Publishing Group, Inc.
29 East 21st Street, New York, NY 10010

First Edition

Editor: Natashya Wilson
Book Design: Kim Sonsky
Layout Design: Emily Muschinske

Illustration Credits: All illustrations © Curt Visca.
Photo Credits: Cover photo (flying fish) p. 20 © Animals Animals/Debble & Stone OSF; cover photo and title page (hand) © Arlan Dean; pp. 6, 12 © Animals Animals/M. Gibbs OSF; p. 8 © Animals Animals/Zig Leszczynski; p. 10 © Animals Animals/Richard Kolar; p. 14 © Animals Animals/Michele Westmorland; p.16 © Animals Animals/Carl Roessler; p. 18 © Animals Animals/Herb Segars.

Visca, Curt.
How to draw cartoon fish / Curt Visca and Kelley Visca.
    p. cm. — (A kid's guide to drawing)
Includes bibliographical references and index.
Summary: Provides facts about different kinds of fish, as well as step-by-step instructions for drawing cartoons of each one.
  ISBN 0-8239-6159-1
1. Cartooning—Technique—Juvenile literature.
2. Fish—Caricatures and cartoons—Juvenile literature. [1. Cartooning—Technique. 2. Fishes in art.] I. Visca, Kelley. II. Title. III. Series.
NC1764.8.F57 V58 2003
  743.6'7—dc21
  2001004327

Manufactured in the United States of America

CONTENTS

Cartoon Fish

Fish are amazing animals that live in **freshwater** and **marine habitats** all around the world. All fish are **vertebrates**, which means they have backbones. They also have **gills**, which are slits behind their eyes that allow them to breathe underwater. Fish use their many types of fins for swimming. **Dorsal fins** stick up from the top of a fish's body. **Pectoral fins** stick out from the sides. **Pelvic fins** and **anal fins** grow from a fish's underside, and a **caudal fin**, or tail fin, makes up the end of a fish. From the more than 40-foot-long (12-m-long) whale shark to the ⅖-inch-long (1-cm-long) goby, fish come in many sizes.

In this book, you will learn interesting facts about eight different fish and how to draw a cartoon of each one. A cartoon drawing includes only basic lines and shapes, keeping it simple. Since the first color cartoon was published in 1893, cartoons have become a popular newspaper feature. A cartoon can be a single drawing in one square or a series of drawings that tell a story in a cartoon strip.

Once you've learned to draw these cartoon fish, you can make your own cartoon strip!

As you draw cartoon fish, you might notice that your fish look different from the ones in the book. That's okay! As a cartoonist, you will develop your own cartooning **style**, or way of drawing. Your style will make your cartoons special.

You will need the following supplies to draw cartoon fish:

- Paper
- A sharp pencil or a felt-tipped marker
- An eraser
- Colored pencils or crayons to add color

Draw your cartoons at a desk, or a table, or in any quiet place with lots of light. Directions under each step will help you add the new parts to your fish. The drawing shapes and terms are listed in Terms for Drawing Cartoons on page 22.

There's something fishy about these cartoons. Turn the page to find out what!

The Angelfish

An angelfish looks graceful when it swims because of its long, slender dorsal and anal fins. Angelfish live in both freshwater and marine habitats. Beautiful freshwater angelfish are often kept in home fish tanks. They come from South America. Marine angelfish live in coral reefs in warm ocean waters. These

brightly colored fish eat **plankton**, worms, and **sea sponges**. Angelfish can be all black, all white, or striped with different colors. Some angelfish are striped yellow and black. Others are silver with dark stripes. Some **species** of angelfish change color as the young become adults.

1

Let's begin by drawing a circle for the right eye. Make a letter C for the top of the mouth. Draw another letter C for the left eye. Place a dot in each eye.

2

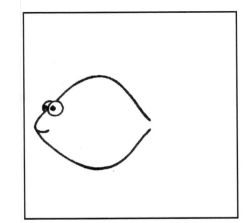

Make a long curved line for the top of the angelfish and a wide letter U for the bottom of the angelfish.

3

Fantastic! Draw two long curved lines, one for the top and one for the bottom of the caudal fin. Make letter C's to connect the fin.

4

Draw a large, upside-down, curved letter V for the dorsal fin and a large, curved letter V for the anal fin.

5

Super! Draw two thin, curved letter V's for the pelvic fins. Add a small, backward letter C for the pectoral fin.

6

Make lines on the fins. Draw bumpy lines and dots for stripes and curved lines for gills. Make seaweed using bent and bumpy lines.

7

The Piranha

Piranhas live in the freshwaters of South America. The meat-eating piranha species are the best known, but some piranhas eat only plants. Piranhas' lower jaws stick

out, making them look mean. They can have up to 27 razor-sharp teeth. Meat-eating piranhas feed on many animals, including fish, insects, and birds. They also eat dead animals. Some piranhas swim alone, and some swim in **schools**. A school of red-bellied piranhas can eat an animal as large as a cow. Red-bellied piranhas have the strongest jaws and the sharpest teeth of any piranha species. When many piranhas eat together, the **prey** can be eaten in seconds. Piranha bites have injured people, but there is no proof that piranhas have ever killed a person.

1

Start by drawing a circle and a backward letter *C* for the eyes. Place a dot in each eye. Make a small line for the top of the mouth. Add a letter *V* above the eyes.

2

Nice job! Draw a sideways letter *V* for the inside of the mouth. Add small letter *V's* and upside-down letter *V's* for the teeth.

3

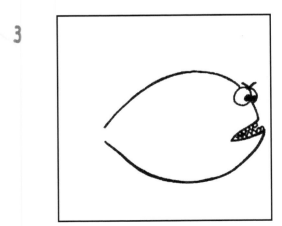

Next make a long curved line for the top of the piranha and a wide letter *U* for the bottom of the piranha.

4

Draw two straight lines for the top and the bottom of the caudal fin. Add a bumpy line to finish the fin.

5

Great work! Make two dorsal fins and an anal fin using straight and bumpy lines. Use a curved wiggly line to make a pectoral fin. Make the pelvic fin using a curved letter *V*.

6

Add circles and dots for scales. Draw curved lines for gills and straight lines in the fins. Make action lines, bubbles, and water.

9

The Goldfish

Goldfish are popular to keep as pets, because they are so easy to care for. Pet goldfish need a fishtank with clean, cold water. A goldfish needs about 1 gallon (4 l) of water for every inch of its length. Most goldfish are from 3 to 5 inches (8–13 cm) long. They can grow as large as 1 foot (30 cm) in length. Some pet goldfish have lived for 50 years, although most live for up to 5 years.

Goldfish are related to the **carp** family and come from Asia. They usually have orange scales, but they can be red, yellow, white, black, silver, or many colors. In the wild, most goldfish are olive green to blend in with their habitat. They eat worms, insects, and plants that they find on the bottoms of ponds.

1

Draw a circle for the right eye. Make a letter C for the top of the mouth. Add a small letter C for the other eye. Draw a dot in each eye.

2

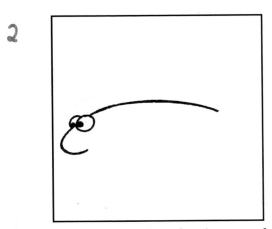

Make a long curved line for the top of your goldfish.

3

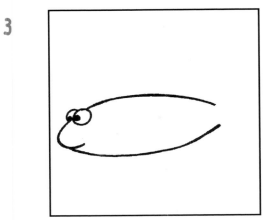

Excellent! Draw a wide letter U for the bottom of the goldfish.

4

Connect two sideways letter U's for the caudal fin.

5

You're awesome! Draw a curved line for the dorsal fin and two letter U's for pelvic and anal fins.

6

Make a pectoral fin, and add lines in the fins. Draw small letter U's for scales and two curved lines for gills. Add action lines, a rocky tank bottom, and water.

The Catfish

Catfish got their name from their catlike whiskers, called **barbels**. These barbels act as feelers, helping catfish find food. They hunt at night and eat whatever they find, including frogs, insects, and dead fish and plants. Most catfish live in freshwater.

Catfish's bodies are covered with smooth skin instead of scales. There are more than 2,000 species of catfish. Some species have **poisonous** spines to keep away **predators**. European catfish can grow to be 10 feet (3 m) long. Blind catfish live in caverns in Pennsylvania. In South America, talking catfish make grunting noises. In Africa, upside-down catfish swim that way. In Asia, walking catfish travel over land to find new bodies of water.

1

Start your catfish with a circle for the left eye. Attach a curved line for the other eye. Make a dot in each eye. Add a short curved line and two upside-down, curved letter V's.

2

Next make a long, curved letter V for the left barbel and another one for the right barbel.

3

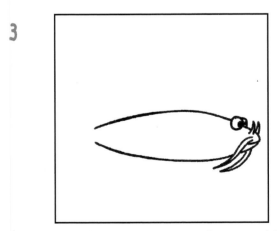

I'm proud of you! Draw a wide curved line for the top of the catfish and a wide letter U for the bottom of the catfish.

4

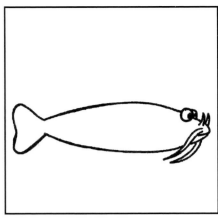

Make two straight lines and connect them with a bent line for the caudal fin.

5

Incredible job! Draw curved lines to make the rest of the fins.

6

Add dots, curved lines for the gills, and straight lines in the fins. Make action lines. Draw a river bottom, weeds, and water bubbles. Wow!

13

The Sea Horse

Sea horses aren't horses at all, but fish with heads shaped like horses heads. Sea horses eat **microorganisms** with their long, toothless mouths. They live in warm ocean waters. Their bodies are covered with hard plates. The heavy plates make sea horses poor swimmers. They use their curled tails to hold on to coral and seaweed so water currents don't sweep them away. Sea horses swim in up-and-down motions using their **transparent** dorsal fins. These fins beat from 20 to 30 times a second, which is so fast that you can't see them! To hide from predators, sea horses can **camouflage** themselves by changing colors. Another great fact about sea horses is that the males carry the eggs until they hatch.

1

Let's start by drawing a circle for the right eye. Draw a letter *C* for the other eye. Place a dot in each eye. Make a long, sideways, wiggly letter *W* for the mouth.

4

Draw a short curved bumpy line for the front of the neck. Attach a wide letter *C* for the stomach. Finish the tail with another curved bumpy line.

2

Make a curved bumpy line for the jaw.

5

Awesome job! Draw the fins on the side of the head and the back of the sea horse with curved lines.

3

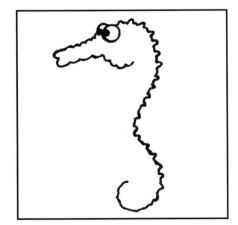

Sensational work! Draw a long curved bumpy line for the back of the sea horse's head, body, and tail.

6

Finish your sea horse by drawing small lines on the fins and detail on the body. Add action lines and seaweed. Nice!

The Clown Fish

Clown fish are brightly striped, orange-and-white fish that live among the **tentacles** of **sea anemones**. These tentacles sting and kill other fish that swim too close to the sea anemones. The sting doesn't bother the clown fish, because the clown fish is protected by a special coating called **mucus**. When a predator chases a clown fish, the clown fish swims into a sea anemone for protection. The clown fish helps the sea anemone by cleaning its tentacles and bringing it food. When two animals help each other survive, like the sea anemone and the clown fish do, that special relationship is called **symbiosis**.

1

Begin by drawing a circle for the left eye. Make a bent line for the top of the mouth. Draw a small, backward letter C for the right eye. Add a dot in each eye.

2

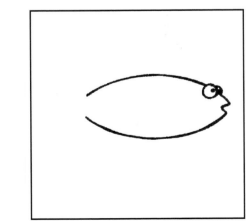

Draw a small letter C for the mouth.

3

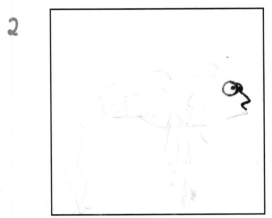

You are doing a terrific job! Draw a long curved line for the top of the clown fish and a wide letter U for the bottom of the clown fish.

4

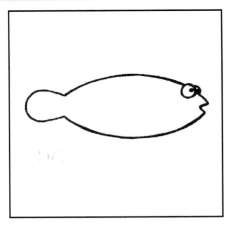

Add two straight lines and a letter C for the caudal fin.

5

Nice work! Draw the letter C for the pectoral fin and curved lines for the other fins.

6

Make bent lines for stripes. Add small lines inside the fins. Draw action lines, circles for bubbles, and sea anemone tentacles.

17

The Puffer

When a predator threatens it, a puffer fills its body with air or water until it looks like a balloon. This makes it very difficult for the predator to swallow the puffer. Puffers can be from 2 to 24 inches (5–61 cm) long. When they puff up, they become about twice their normal size. When not puffed up, puffers are oval shaped. They have smooth, leathery skin. A puffer's teeth are **fused**, or stuck, together. They form a mouth that looks like a bird's beak. Puffers use their hard mouths to eat shellfish and coral.

Many species of puffers are poisonous. Puffers are considered a **delicacy** in Japan. They must be cooked in a special way to make them safe to eat. There is no cure for a puffer's poison. Eating a puffer can cause death if the fish is not cooked correctly!

1

Start by drawing a circle for the right eye. Add a bent line for the front of the puffer. Make a letter C for the other eye. Draw a dot in each eye.

2

Draw two small, connected letter C's for the mouth.

3

You did it! Make a long curved line for the top of the puffer and a wide letter U for the bottom.

4

Make a curved line for the caudal fin.

5

Outstanding! Draw an upside-down letter U for the dorsal fin, a sideways letter U for the anal fin, and a curved wiggly line for the pectoral fin on the side of the puffer.

6

Add detail to your incredible puffer. Make small lines inside the fins. Draw a curved line for a gill, and add action lines.

The Flying Fish

Flying fish got their name because they can leap up to 36 feet (11 m) out of the water and glide as far as 600 feet (183 m) through the air. A flying fish builds up speed under the water, then uses its powerful caudal fin to push itself out of the water. It glides through the air using its long, stiff pectoral fins, which look like wings. Flying fish leap out of the water when they are being followed by predators, such as bluefish and tuna.

Flying fish live in warm ocean waters. The largest flying fish are found off the California coast. They can grow to be up to 18 inches (46 cm) long.

1

Begin by drawing a circle and an upside-down letter *U* for the eyes. Add dots. Make a curved line for the front of the head.

2

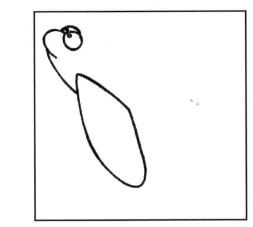

Draw a slightly curved line for the bottom of the flying fish.

3

Splendid work! Draw a large, curved letter *U* and a straight line for the stiff pectoral fin of the flying fish.

4

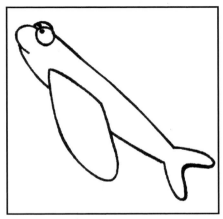

Make a long straight line for the top of the flying fish. Draw a short straight line for the underside of the flying fish. Connect two sideways letter *U*'s for the caudal fin.

5

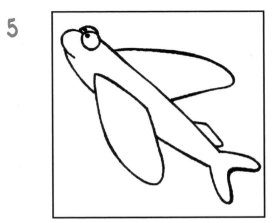

Terrific work! Draw a long curved line for the other pectoral fin and three straight lines for the dorsal fin.

6

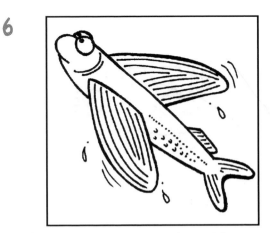

Finish your super cartoon by adding detail, curved lines for gills, lines in the fins, action lines, and teardrops for splashing water.

Terms for Drawing Cartoons

Here are some of the words and shapes that you will need to draw cartoon fish:

((	Action lines	C	Letter C
∫	Bent line	⁞	Small letter U's
O	Circle	≡	Small lines
◡	Curved bumpy line	│	Straight line
⪽	Curved letter V	◊	Teardrop
⌒	Curved line	‿	Wide letter U
3	Curved wiggly line	⧂	Wiggly letter W
ℰ∴	Detail		
∴	Dots		

Glossary

anal fins (AY-nul FINZ) Fins that grow under a fish, near the tail.

barbels (BAR-belz) Thin feelers by the mouths of catfish.

camouflage (KA-muh-flaj) To hide by a pattern that matches one's background.

carp (KARP) A group of freshwater fish from Asia that shares similar traits.

caudal fin (KAW-dul FIN) Tail fin.

delicacy (DEH-lih-kuh-see) Something pleasing to eat that is uncommon.

dorsal fins (DOR-sul FINZ) Fins on top of a fish's back.

freshwater (FRESH-wah-ter) Water without salt.

fused (FYOOZD) Joined together.

gills (GILZ) Slits behind the heads of fish through which they breathe.

habitats (HA-bih-tats) Surroundings where animals or plants naturally live.

marine (muh-REEN) Having to do with the sea or salt water.

microorganisms (my-kroh-OR-guh-nih-zuhmz) Tiny living things.

mucus (MYOO-kus) A slimy coating that makes a surface slippery.

pectoral fins (PEK-tur-ul FINZ) The fins on the sides of a fish.

pelvic fins (PEL-vihk FINZ) Fins that grow on the underside of a fish, toward its front.

plankton (PLANK-ten) Plants and animals that drift with water currents.

poisonous (POY-zun-is) Able to make you very sick or to kill you.

predators (PREH-duh-terz) Animals that hunt other animals for food.

prey (PRAY) An animal that another animal wants to eat.

schools (SKOOLZ) Large groups of fish.

sea anemones (SEE uh-NEH-muh-neez) Brightly colored sea animals that look like flowers.

sea sponges (SEE SPUN-jez) Squishy sea animals that stick to rocks.

species (SPEE-sheez) A group of animals that share similar characteristics.

style (STYL) A special way of acting or looking that makes a person who he or she is.

symbiosis (sim-bee-OH-sis) When two animals help each other to survive.

tentacles (TEN-tuh-kuhlz) Long, thing growths usually on the head or near the mouths of animals, used to touch, hold, or move.

transparent (tranz-PAYR-ent) Able to be seen through.

vertebrates (VER-tih-brits) Animals that have backbones.

Index

Web Sites

To learn more about fish, check out these Web sites:

http://endangered.fws.gov/kids/kid_cor.htm
www.ncdmf.net/kids/fish.htm
www.tropicalfish.com/html/kids_page.html

24